W9-BYN-627

In Lviv only

Roaming around the ancient town

 2003

Lviv is your city as well!

It would appear that amid the overabundance
of stories told about Lviv further eulogizing
it is nothing short of impossible.
It would appear that enough has been said.
Nothing can be farther from the truth.
The princely town is insatiable; craving ever so renewed
attention, time and again luring new guests,
not hiding from them behind age-old mysteries.
This time Lviv has enlisted the services
of two more of its aides, namely Oles Hanushchak
and Yosyf Marukhnyak, authors of the illustrated
guidebook, In Lviv only. On their part,
they have thrown wide a new gateway to Lviv,
through which they usher those eager to learn
about the birthplace of Prince Lev (Leo).
It opens with the Dvirets, the railway station.
Unlike their predecessors, the authors offer
a quite out-of-the-way outing.
The itinerary is far from easy and yet picturesque:
prepare for a beer-guzzling, coffee-savoring,
and chocolate-eating experience.
Be ready to spare some loose change for buskers
or beggars, see trams rattle crosstown,
minibuses squeeze through the rush-hour traffic,
Shevchenko frown upon the bustling crowd,
hear Mickiewicz bandy words with his muse
and chimes from the City Hall Tower herald
the end of yet another day...
This is Lviv!
Beyond doubt, the present work will find its due place
on Lviv's scholarly shelves and will measure up to tributes
given it in the days past and the ones still to come.

Yaroslav DASHKEVYCH, *chief scientific adviser*
Bohdan MYKHALYUNYO, *scientific adviser*

Contents

First impressions
4
From the terminal and into the pub
5
Under the auspices of Saint George
10
From Jesuits to Kamenyar
12
Names on the stone
15
Picture Gallery, Palace of the Potocki, Mickiewicz...
19
Hrushevskyy and Lyudkevych would stroll Akademichna Street
24
On knights, muses, and liberty on Svobody Avenue
27
«There in Lviv, in Rynok Square...»
34
Armenian and Ruthenian Streets, Dominicans...
42
Gothic, Turkish cannonballs, and human ambition
50
Bernardinian's trace, Arsenal Museum
52
Gunpowder Tower, democracy, and lions
56
On the Castle Hill
58
Public transportation, taxis
60
Hotels, restaurants, cafes
62
Money, payments, banks
64

4

First impressions

Most historians, ethnographers, fine arts experts, or rank-and-file enthusiasts of Lviv are in the habit of starting their narrative tour of Lviv with the city's very heartland, Rynok Square (Marketplace) or Vysokyy Zamok (Castle Hill). This is only natural, as it is arguably the best way to make the traveling guest fall in love with the Renaissance exquisiteness of Rynok Square or impress him with breathtaking vistas opening up from the Castle Hill. It is not accidental that Lviv has been designated a UNESCO world heritage site.

Not for the sake of originality alone, which our city and its inhabitants have been amply endowed with, we will begin our narration of Lviv, its illustrious history, flamboyant residents who know dozens of amazing legends about their city, from the railway station.

Passing by picturesque grassy hillocks on a refreshingly cool morning the train is slowly approaching the railway gateway to Halychyna (Galicia), the oldest and, owing to modern Lviv residents, the most up-to-date railway terminal in Western Ukraine. All in all, there are eight approaches to the modern Lviv, including the bus terminal, airport, and, of course, the Dvirets (derived from Polish dworzec for railway station). Precisely, conservative Lvivites still call their railway station that, and rightly so...

From the terminal and into the pub

True to the famed medieval traditions, Lviv was duly considered one of the biggest trading centers in the Austrian Empire until the mid-19th century, which it was then a part of. A teeming marketplace would every so often spread out at the foot of the St. George's Hill (where the Saint George Cathedral now stands). City fathers chose the pasture, where the railway terminal was eventually built, as the best place for the merchants and guests of those days arriving for the fair.

In 1861, when the first train from Przemysl rumbled along on its way to Lviv, sending out clouds of smoke and steam, hundreds of awestruck suburban peasants and residents of artisan neighborhoods were eying it suspiciously. First passengers, a few respectable messieurs and two dozen small traders, entered a squatty wooden building.

At the turn of the 19th century, in the Austrian Empire Lviv was commonly referred to as the capital of backward province, a haven for hapless functionaries, adventurers, and impoverished noblemen heading there to pursue a career, make a fast buck, or wait through bad times.

Even at that time it was true only partly. Otherwise, Lviv would not have become the metropolis of the Kingdom of Halychyna and Volodymyriya which was part of the empire. In geographic and cultural terms Lviv has been always considered a lively bridge connecting the East and West; in economic terms it was a sort of melting pot and pump of money, merchandise, services, and news. Such an exchange would not have been possible if it was not for the

railway and the imposing terminal. Designed by Sadlovskyy, it was erected in 1904. The railway terminal stood in flames three times under various circumstances. Partially destroyed by Luftwaffe bombs on the first day of World War II, it was ravaged in 1944 by American Air Force. After numerous facelifts, it was eventually renovated and modernized in 2001. Now it is credited with being one of the most imposing railway terminals in Ukraine and is unhurriedly preparing to celebrate its centennial.

6

While the cabman is loading your baggage into the boot or you are carrying it yourself to the nearby municipal tram or the so-called route minibus, let me say a few words about Lvivites. Ever since the early Middle Ages, Lviv had been more or less successfully ruled by Halychyna and Volyn kings and princes, Polish and Hungarian kings, Rzhecz-pospolita, Austro-Hungary, Poland again, the Soviet Empire... The ever-changing powers and cultural influences have left an indelible imprint not only on the city architecture, but also on the way of life, habits, traditions, and the inhabitants' vernacular. The flamboyant patois of Lviv residents is studded with Polish, German, and Russian words which lend special charm to the Ukrainian language. With a small exception, Lvivites speak Ukrainian at work and at home, most Lviv's Armenians, Poles, Hungarians, Jews, and Russians speak Ukrainian fluently...

Lviv residents spend most of their free time savoring coffee and, let's give them their due, are a recognized authority on it. A few legends have been perpetuated about how the exotic beverage from the East turned up in Lviv. Twice laying siege to Lviv, Hetman Bohdan Khmelnytskyy would refresh himself with Arabic coffee for which he developed a liking while in captivity in Turkey. Or maybe one of the Lvivites participating in the Battle of Vienna brought this wonderworking booty home... Or maybe some Polish noble, bought out from Turkish captivity, made it off with a pouch of coffee... Be that as it may, coffee has been part of a daily routine in Lviv for a number of centuries. This has become a veritable cult. Business negotiations, dating, leisurely talks of daily life... everything happens over a cup of coffee. Black coffee is mostly drunk, usually in one's favorite coffee shops. Traditions come first...

In the course of our tour we will miss neither Lviv coffee shops, nor famed Lviv beer, nor the matchless sweets of Sweetouch... But let us start *ab ovo*, that is, from where we set out.

The map our guide, we make it from the terminal under overhanging crowns of age-old trees of Chernivetska Street onto Horodotska Street. This road would always take people to a picturesque township of Horodok in the direction of Poland. Now it will take you to the Ukrainian-Polish customs border crossing of Shehyni. But so far we are headed elsewhere. Let us make a left turn from the terminal. The first thing to catch the eye are steep majestic spires towering above rooftops. That is Church of Elisabeth. From the architectural viewpoint, this exaggerated edifice deserves only a passing mention. It was built in the neo-gothic style. Yet Lviv's Catholics hold their church dear, renovate and cherish it. Much remains to be renovated, as during the Soviet era the local authorities used it as a makeshift storehouse for construction materials.

Lvivites perpetuated a sad, yet romantic legend about the Church of Elisabeth. In September 1898, Empress Elisabeth, wife of the Austrian Emperor, died during her vacation at Lake Geneva in Switzerland. She was slain by anarchist Luigi Luccani. To immortalize the name of the deceased Empress, Lvivites collected donations and used them to build the Roman Catholic Church of St. Elżbieta (Elizabeth) which to this day impresses city guests with its neo-gothic openwork.

8

Should you wish to proceed down Horodotska Street, you wi[ll] hardly see anything outstanding or noteworthy. It would b[e] stretching to call a monument of architecture the overturne[d] «cauldron» of the circus built in the Soviet fashion. Only th[e] St. George Cathedral is picturesquely towering above it. Y[ou] farther down the road, at the junction of Shevchenko (former[ly] Yanivska Street) and Horodotska Streets you can stop to as[k] directions to Kleparivska Street. The hillock to the left [of] Kleparivska Street used to serve as a site of public execution[s] while to the right passions would run high and still do. That [is] where Krakivskyy market is. Although far from Lviv's bigge[st] and best, it's one of the oldest local markets. The market has a[ll] attributes of post-Soviet «capitalism». Notably, there is Lviv[s] only pet market. Should you want to buy a puppy or kitten wi[th] an astounding, albeit bogus, pedigree, be my guest.

t the end of Kleparivska Street there is
viv's pride and joy, Ukraine's oldest
viv Brewery. Beer has been brewed
ithin its redbrick walls ever since 1715.
owever, brewers were known to have lived
Lviv long before that. Thus, in 1527
e whole town burnt down in a fire that
oke out in a brewery in Frantsyskanska
reet. Some may as well be surprised to
arn that in good old times Lviv-made
er would be exported to ... Bavaria.
ow do you like that?

he fact that the quality and unmatched
avor of Lviv-made beer have not
eteriorated over centuries can be best
scertained in the vaults of the brewery's
er restaurant, Zolotyy Kolos (Golden
arley Ear). By and large, brewing
aditions in Lviv date from the Middle
ges. Breweries were owned by monks,

merchants, and town authorities. The brewers'
guild would thoroughly monitor the quality
of beer. Its quality was put to the test in a
quite peculiar way. A mugful of beer would
be spilt all over the oak bench. A brewer in
leather pants would then sit on the wet bench.
In a while, he would get to his feet. The bench
had to stick to his pants so as not to fall off
when he stood up...

And although beer of any sorts is on offer in
Lviv, Lviv-made beer is the choice of true
connoisseurs and supporters. Whether it's
light, dark, Premium, or strong is a matter of
taste. Enjoy!

Under the auspices of Saint George

Having emptied a mugful of good Lviv beer, leisurely return to the cauldron-like circus from where steep Ozarkevycha Street goes up to St. George Hill. It will take you past the Greek-Catholic charitable hospital named after Metropolitan Andrey Sheptytskyy right to the St. George Square at the gates of the St. George Cathedral. While we proceed, let me say a few words about Sheptytskyy. A genteel officer of the Austro-Hungarian Army, he devoted himself to serving God while still a young man. He was the Metropolitan of the Greek-Catholic Church during its hardest times of the first Bolshevik occupation of the city and World War II. A noted scholar, philosopher, philanthropist, and public figure, he was buried in the crypt of the St. George Cathedral.

The origin of the Cathedral of St. George is the subject of a number of legends. According to one of them, here, hidden among blackthorn bushes, was a cave where Prince Voyshelk settled in 1280. Well into his twilight years, he sought redemption of sins in prayer and took his monastic vows. Upon his request Prince Lev built a beech church and cells for monks. Another legend says the church had in fact been built by Prince George himself. Over time it had become a real monastery surrounded by a moat and palisade. Since at that time the monastery and cathedral were outside the city walls, they were essentially seen as the town's defense outpost. Notably, the monks inhabiting this citadel quite skillfully wielded swords, axes, and maces.

In 1655, the St. George Hill was the site of Bohdan Khmelnytskyy's encampment. The flag of the Ukrainian host was hoisted on the church belfry. It was in the Church of St. George where Bohdan Khmelnytskyy received Bishop Zhelyborskyy as well as the ambassador from King Kazimierz who tried to talk him into signing an armistice. The Hetman's headquarters were next to the church and close by was the Chancellery of General Clerk Vyhovskyy.

Engineer B. Meretyn and famed sculptor Y. Pinzel are credited with shaping much of the cathedral's current appearance in 1744—1761.

Now the Cathedral of St. George is the best monument of Baroque architecture in Ukraine. Apart from the cathedral, the architectural ensemble comprises the belfry, capital, Metropolitan's Chambers, garden, and the surrounding wall. No other building in the city can boast such an unparalleled combination of elaborate decorative carvings and architecture. The only eyesore is the grotesque tower, a leftover of the Soviet-time construction binge. They say it was a radio waves jammer intended to prevent people from tuning in to the Voice of America. Word has it, to dismantle this miscreation now would be more costly and dangerous than it was to build it.

During his sojourn in Lviv in 2001 Pope John Paul II stayed in the Metropolitan Chambers of the Cathedral. Currently, while the construction of modern premises is under way in Kyiv, His Beatitude, Metropolitan of the Greek-Catholic Church Lyubomyr Cardinal Huzar lives and works in the Chambers. Though being advanced in years, he receives visitors every day and is actively involved in charity and educational programs. Guests are welcome to visit the Cathedral and its premises.

From Jesuits to Kamenyar

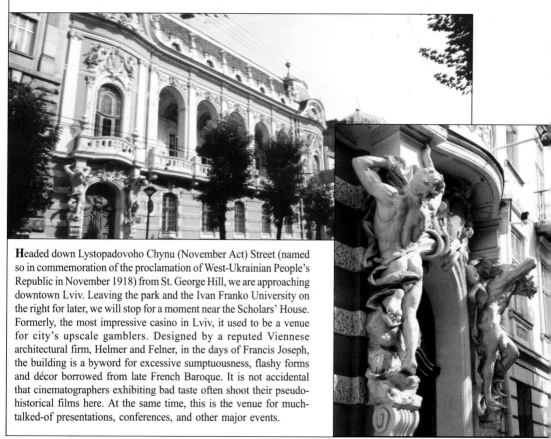

Headed down Lystopadovoho Chynu (November Act) Street (named so in commemoration of the proclamation of West-Ukrainian People's Republic in November 1918) from St. George Hill, we are approaching downtown Lviv. Leaving the park and the Ivan Franko University on the right for later, we will stop for a moment near the Scholars' House. Formerly, the most impressive casino in Lviv, it used to be a venue for city's upscale gamblers. Designed by a reputed Viennese architectural firm, Helmer and Felner, in the days of Francis Joseph, the building is a byword for excessive sumptuousness, flashy forms and décor borrowed from late French Baroque. It is not accidental that cinematographers exhibiting bad taste often shoot their pseudo-historical films here. At the same time, this is the venue for much-talked-of presentations, conferences, and other major events.

he Ivan Franko National University. This educational institution ranks among Ukraine's oldest ones. ounded in Lviv in 1661, the university moved into the present main building much later, namely in 1920. the second half of the 19th century Lviv became the capital of the Province of Halychyna in Austro-ungary. Thus, apart from other administrative establishments, the premises of the Seym of Halychyna cal representative authority) were built at this site (architect Hochberger). Now they house the main uilding of the university. In keeping with the notions of grandeur and beauty of those days, the uilding has been imparted a monumental appearance in the style of the late Italian Renaissance. The çade of the central building is especially imposing. It is crowned with symbolic figures of Halychyna, e Dniester, and the Vistula. Below them, on either side of the central entrance are statuary groups mbolizing Education and Labor.

ineffaceable Soviet times, monuments to Lenin opposite the Opera House and anko facing the university were dubbed Lviv's major architectural symbols. Both re seen as the epitome of Soviet fundamentalism and obsession with Cyclopean nstruction. Unlike Lenin, dethroned and toppled by Lvivites, Franko has remained e luminary of Ukrainian and world cultures. The monument has been preserved, sculptural shortcomings notwithstanding. The more so that the square near Franko is the site of protest rallies staged by national democratic forces struggling for kraine's independence. These rallies would be every so often broken up by the gressive Communist authorities only to resume with more vigor, which provided impetus to all Ukrainian progressive forces to fight for sovereignty and democracy.

Behind the broad shoulders of Kamenyar (I.Franko, the Stone-breaker) stretches a picturesque an shaded park named after himself (formerly the Jesuits' Park). Before the park there used to be t town's pasture, which later was under private ownership. Over time, the land was appropriated Jesuits. The monks, whose end justified the means, built a brickyard, brewery, and... a tavern. Th hired workers to attend to their lucrative business.

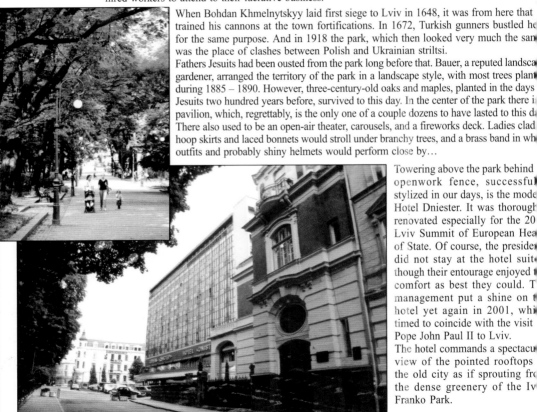

When Bohdan Khmelnytskyy laid first siege to Lviv in 1648, it was from here that trained his cannons at the town fortifications. In 1672, Turkish gunners bustled he for the same purpose. And in 1918 the park, which then looked very much the sam was the place of clashes between Polish and Ukrainian striltsi.

Fathers Jesuits had been ousted from the park long before that. Bauer, a reputed landsca gardener, arranged the territory of the park in a landscape style, with most trees plant during 1885 – 1890. However, three-century-old oaks and maples, planted in the days Jesuits two hundred years before, survived to this day. In the center of the park there i pavilion, which, regrettably, is the only one of a couple dozens to have lasted to this da There also used to be an open-air theater, carousels, and a fireworks deck. Ladies clad hoop skirts and laced bonnets would stroll under branchy trees, and a brass band in wh outfits and probably shiny helmets would perform close by…

Towering above the park behind openwork fence, successfu stylized in our days, is the mode Hotel Dniester. It was thorough renovated especially for the 20 Lviv Summit of European Hea of State. Of course, the preside did not stay at the hotel suit though their entourage enjoyed comfort as best they could. T management put a shine on hotel yet again in 2001, wh timed to coincide with the visit Pope John Paul II to Lviv.

The hotel commands a spectacu view of the pointed rooftops the old city as if sprouting fr the dense greenery of the Iv Franko Park.

Names on the stone

From the park's upper edge we make it via Solomiyi Krushelnytskoyi Street, where the famous singer used to live (a commemorative plaque on the corner reminds about that), via short Kamenyariv Street onto Doroshenka Street. Rightwards and further up we find ourselves in Stepana Bandery Street.

The story of how this street came by this name is indicative of the set of mind and views of Halychyna people. Even before independence, Lviv deputies, defying the pressure from the Communist authorities, named this street, which begins under the walls of the building that used to house the infamous NKVD (the Soviet government's secret police) and where thousands of patriots had been tortured to death, in the honor of the leader of Ukraine's National Liberation Movement, Stepan Bandera. Opposite the forbidding building, a monument to victims of the Bolshevik regime was unveiled in 1997. Sculptor — Shtayer, architect — Syvenkyy.

Before World War I, this square belonged to the local Ukrainian community who had plans to build here a Ukrainian theater. Talk of quirks of fate!

The building at 1 Bandery Street currently houses the municipal constabulary. Word has it, young police lieutenants working night shifts can hear moans and curses from the dungeons which used to be the NKVD prison.

Not turning our back on history, let us turn away from the grim and sinister building. Above, there is heavenly music, history, and beauty, the former Roman-Catholic Church of St. Mary Magdalene, a splendid monument of early Lviv Baroque of the 17th century. Designed by local architects Hornyy and Kelar, it was later reconstructed by Urbanyk. It was then that Baroque sculptures bedecked the façade of the church, which, experts believe, are harmonious with the style of the church.

Currently, the church accommodates the House of Chamber and Organ Music. The sounds coming out of the ancient organ are as clear and elevated as three centuries ago. Should you chance upon a concert, it is sure to make an indelible impression on you.

16

If you again walk past the municipal constabulary farther down, you w come onto Copernicus Street (Kopernika Street). Merits of this Polis astronomer have not been questioned by any of the powers, thus th street, Lviv's straightest, has been bearing this name for quite a long tim Let us stop for a moment near the fountain with lions once s successfully embedded into the hillside. It's not ruled out that pristi water used to flow into the fountain bowl and passersby could slal their thirst for free. You won't taste that water, as the spring has drie up, while the fountain and lions have been disfigured by ravages time and people. Perhaps someone did find out the name of the auth of this humble monument but so far is keeping the secret to himself

A hundred steps down and to the left you will s a striking edifice, either a chateau or a mansio This miracle of a building used to belong to a not family of the Ukrainians-tuned-Poles Sapyeh The plaque reads that this stylish building currently housing the local Association for t Protection of Historical Memorials. There something symbolic in the fact that the buildin is deteriorating.

Close by there is a lone belfry in a square fenc in by featureless edifices of the second half of t previous century. Before World War II, there use to be a Greek-Catholic Seminary whose rector w Yosyp Slipyy, a renowned religious and cultur figure. A stele on the sidewall of the city Ma Post Office is a reminder of those days.

МАРКІЯН ШАШКЕВИЧ

Markiyan Shashkevych, another luminary of Ukrainian culture, founder of the writers' circle Ruska Triytsya, and author of Rusalka Dnistrova (Mermaid of the Dniester) almanac, graduated from this seminary. In his student days there used to be a big garden and dwellings for students and servants at the site of the modern post office. Windows facing the street had gratings on them. Probably ever since then an amusing tale spread by word of mouth. Once some villager stopped to stare at the grated window. A student from within started mocking him, to which he retorted: «Keep laughing. If you were a decent fellow, you wouldn't have been placed behind bars». During the 1941 Nazi air raid on Lviv, only a few heavy aviation bombs were dropped. Regrettably, this proved enough to raze to the ground both the church and the seminary. Only the belfry survived. And next to it a monument to Markiyan Shashkevych was erected in our days. Maybe someday the church complex and fragments of the seminary will be rebuilt as a hub of Ukrainian culture and the spirit of enlightenment in Halychyna.

17

18

To the right of the junction of Copernicus Stre[et] and the tree-shaded Stefanyka Street there is t[he] commanding Scientific Library named for Vasyl St[e]fanyk. If you are not aware of this fact, he was th[e] writer about whom they would say: «How incisive[,]» laconically, and dauntingly that man writes...»

Getting back to the building, at this very site the[re] used to be the Roman-Catholic Church [of] Barefooted Carmelites, which had been eventuall[y] shut down. In 1780-90s, Lviv architecture wa[s] dominated by the style of classicism. Incidentall[y] the building of Stefanyk Library (before 1939 [it] housed the Institute named for the Ossolinski [or] «Ossolineum») is to date regarded an unparallele[d] monument of classicism in architecture. I[ts] elements are well-balanced and proportionate. [In] the center of the façade there is a light portico wi[th] a fronton supported with Corinthian pilasters. Th[e] right wing is rounded off with a dome on a sol[id] cylindrical bedding.

Picture Gallery,
Palace of the Potocki, Mickewicz...

A Polish dependency from 1918 through 1939, Halychyna escaped Bolshevik and Stalinist cultural repressions. For this reason, Lviv has preserved the richest collections of books and works of art in Ukraine, while in the Ukrainian land at that time belonging to the USSR 80 percent of the cultural heritage was destroyed. Lviv is the home to more than half Ukraine's architectural monuments.

The Picture Gallery is a graphic example of Lviv's special cultural status. It opened back in 1907 with a collection of paintings and sculptures by West European artists, which the city council bought from private collectors. The gallery has almost never been robbed since it opened. In the 1980s, a few works surfaced in private collections, which were reported missing from repositories in late 1940s after visits by «excursionists» from the NKVD. They emerged in hideaways of their descendants but have ever since disappeared as mysteriously.

It was in our days, when the gallery was blatantly robbed and two of its workers killed. Neither the burglars, nor the stolen things have been found. Unprecedented security measures were taken in the wake of the burglary.

Until recently, a mere ten percent of the stock of masterpieces could be put on display in the spacious hallways of the gallery. The rest were crammed in the repositories. Now the problem has been largely solved, as the gallery is to move to the premises of the nearby Palace of the Potocki, a hundred steps down the Copernicus Street past the modern Arts Palace.

This area used to be dominated by swamps and backwaters of the Poltva River. An aristocratic Polish family of the Potocki, many of whom were reputed to be habitual hunters, came by this place where they built a hunter's shack. Wild ducks were flying right under its windows. Over time, the hunter's hut had grown into a chic mansion where Polish gentry and guests from abroad would give lavish banquets. Ever since then, only once the villa-turned-palace of the Potocki was in real danger.

In the late 1980s, Soviet city fathers busied themselves with building a subway in Lviv. One of the junction terminals was to be built right under the palace. The enthusiasts of cyclopean construction overlooked the fact that swampy grounds of Poltva's backwaters were still there, only enclosed in stone. The palace had a narrow escape when the construction was put on hold and tunnels were backfilled.

According to latest available data, the palace was built in 1880 in French classicism style (architects Tsybulskyy and Overn). The sumptuousness of architecture and décor had considerably worn off during the time it was occupied by the so-called Palace of Ceremonial Events, or, put simply, the registrar's office. Kyiv moguls had plans to turn the Palace of the Potocki into a West Ukrainian residence of the president. But, word has it, it dawned on one of them before it was too late that to do that would be too costly, while the chief executive of the state would not feel very much at home in the midst of a populous city. Eventually, city fathers have handed the palace over to the Picture Gallery. Lord be praised for that!

It needs to be mentioned, however, that the palace has suites fitted out especially to accommodate VIPs. It is common practice the world over and, in all probability, it is lucrative.

If we head down Copernicus Street, we will reach the very heartland of Lviv, Adam Mickiewicz Square. As we proceed, we will see buildings of more or less architectural or historical value, just like anywhere in Lviv. One of the classics used to live here, there someone attempted to hurl a bomb at the governor, close by in the cellar (or attic) there is the studio of a contemporary famous artist... A concise guidebook cannot possibly cover all of the noteworthy facts or events, because old Lviv, as they say, is a legend in itself, a book on history, a tragedy and anecdote. In a word, it is a solid time stratum in which the Lvivites live and, mind you, do not suffer from megalomania, though the feeling of self-esteem runs high here.

Roughly where Mickewicz Square now is, two tributaries of the Poltva River, rivulets Pasika (Ukrainian for Apiary) and Soroka (Magpie), converged in the 15th century. In the middle of the river there was an isle on which devout Lvivites erected a figurine of Virgin Mary. She is still where she was, though there is no trace of the rivers and swamps. Incidentally, water used to be in abundant supply in those days. Word has it, in times of major flooding the Poltva would cause great damage, and two watermills were working energetically next to the Isle of Virgin Mary.

The monument to Adam Mickiewicz, designed by noted sculptors Popel and Parashchuk, has been towering above the square since 1905. A poetical luminary, Mickiewicz cuts a spectacular figure in Polish culture. The sculptors managed to accentuate precisely this in the posture of the poet, who is inspiredly conversing with his muse. The monument has been such a success that the Poles still contemplate relocating it to Warsaw or elsewhere in Poland. Incidentally, the Austro-Hungarian imperial power, commonly regarded as aggressive and undemocratic, had no objections to the symbol of Polish patriotism being erected in downtown Lviv. Not everything is as simple and black-and-white as history books paint it. Lviv is graphic evidence of this.

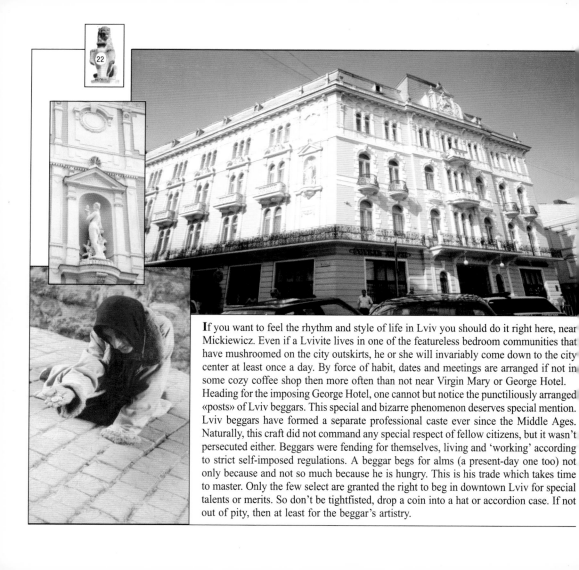

If you want to feel the rhythm and style of life in Lviv you should do it right here, near Mickiewicz. Even if a Lvivite lives in one of the featureless bedroom communities that have mushroomed on the city outskirts, he or she will invariably come down to the city center at least once a day. By force of habit, dates and meetings are arranged if not in some cozy coffee shop then more often than not near Virgin Mary or George Hotel. Heading for the imposing George Hotel, one cannot but notice the punctiliously arranged «posts» of Lviv beggars. This special and bizarre phenomenon deserves special mention. Lviv beggars have formed a separate professional caste ever since the Middle Ages. Naturally, this craft did not command any special respect of fellow citizens, but it wasn't persecuted either. Beggars were fending for themselves, living and 'working' according to strict self-imposed regulations. A beggar begs for alms (a present-day one too) not only because and not so much because he is hungry. This is his trade which takes time to master. Only the few select are granted the right to beg in downtown Lviv for special talents or merits. So don't be tightfisted, drop a coin into a hat or accordion case. If not out of pity, then at least for the beggar's artistry.

At different times there were famous beggars respected by the community. A former handsome officer who had gone clean through his inheritance in brothels and casinos. An old man who would pose for student painters for a bottle of vodka, but never got drunk. But the fate of Yuzyo the Lipnyk (Sticker) is arguably the most amazing.

The man had a weakness. He would spend all the money he could make on lottery tickets. He pledged to quit playing with fate and stuck the last ticket he bought to the door to his own apartment. Imagine his dismay when this proved to be the winning ticket. Not to damage the precious slip of paper, the Sticker unhinged the door and took it to the lottery office. The dumbfounded clerk didn't know where to paste the door with the ticket. Moreover, it turned out that the ticket was not winning after all. Grief-stricken Yuzyo returned home together with the door only to see that his apartment had been robbed clean. Ever since there had been one more beggar in Lviv.

And the renovated George Hotel is right before us. With its suites, restaurant, and casino, it has always been a hotel here. It has had its ups and downs. The façade is crowned with a grand bas-relief of St. George killing the dragon, who, it may seem, has been eternally fighting all human sins. Along its perimeter the building is adorned with allegoric figures of Europe, Asia, Africa, and America.

George Hotel was in its heyday in the 19th century when card-playing became the latest fad across Europe. Cards were played everywhere, in coffee shops, at home, in casinos and restaurants. Europe's celebrated card players would come to Lviv for the gambling season. There were local aces, too. Maestro Stanislav Lyudkevych was a recognized preference player. Word has it, there was only one way you could win from Lyudkevych, alias Syas. In the course of the game one of those present would start singing out of tune, which irritated and made the noted composer nervous. When the maestro's criticism fell on deaf ears, Lyudkevych would lose his bearings and sometimes lose the game. Old waiters at George Restaurant still remember that, even when advanced in years, the maestro would come to George from the Conservatoire, which is close by, right on the dot for lunch. He would sit at 'his' table set with the whitest of tablecloths, order coffee and a cupful of good cognac to go with it. Lyudkevych would always take the time to count off a tip for the waiter.

A motley crowd of Lviv Bohemia, politicians, artists, businessmen, illicit foreign currency dealers, journalists, still stop by at George for a cup of coffee. Experienced bartenders don't even ask their regulars how many lumps of sugar they want in their coffee, or what cognac or liquor they prefer. Traditions, you know...

Hrushevskyy and Lyudkevych would stroll Akademichna Street

Having emptied a cup of coffee at George Hotel we proceed to Akademichna Street, now known as Shevchenka Avenue.

Since the broad avenue is bisected by a trim parkway and cars run only in one direction, we will also follow this route.

Getting back to the parkway, after the Poltva had been enclosed in stone and hidden underground, the parkway was planted where it used to flow. At first curly poplars were lining the street, but they had either grown old or bothered Lvivites with their fluff, and that's why young trees have replaced them.

And to the right, building No. 8 houses the bookstore of the Taras Shevchenko Scholarly Association, which opened here back in 1892. Under changing political regimes, various establishments occupied the bookstore. Eventually in the mid-1990s Ukrainian bibliophiles smoked out of there a tobacco shop. The bookstore offers the widest selection of Ukrainian-language literature everything from ABCs to academic publications.

Close by are glittering storefronts of a neo-Baroque confectionery of the Sweetouch company. Here you will find everything manufactured by Lviv's flagship sweets maker. And in the basement there is a spacious coffee shop.

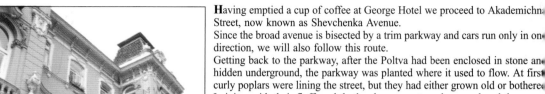

The specialty of the bar is that it is adorned with original lanterns, work of Andriy Bokotey, currently the rector of the Academy of Arts. In Soviet times, there was a dessert bar, a venue for local jazz enthusiasts. Now these jazz veterans can be seen playing near George Hotel.

Guardsmen on the lookout and a row of gleaming cars of foreign makes are an indication that the nigh club Sophia is within reach. During one visit to the club you can part with a few hundred dollars without too much trouble and get a fair measure of life's amenities and pleasures in return. Before the club there used to be Lviv's best bathhouse and before that the bathhouse of St. Anna.

The avenue ends with a picturesque square where Ukraine's first President Mykhaylo Hrushevskyy is seated on a solid footing. Sculptors: Krvavych, Posikira, Yaremchuk. Architect: Kamenetskyy. The monument was erected some years ago and its location is not accidental. Behind the right shoulder of the president there is the Cathedral of the Protection of the Virgin (Svyatoyi Pokrovy), formerly Saint Nicholas Cathedral. Close by there is one of the numerous buildings of the Ivan Franko National University where Professor Hrushevskyy lectured from 1984 through 1910.

Walking back to George Hotel on the opposite side of the avenue, we stop for a moment near the imposing façade of a building that formerly housed the commodities and stock exchange and now is the regional prosecutor's office. This place conjures up sad memories of a tragedy that occurred here not that long ago. In May 2000, Ukraine's famous songwriter and national artist Ihor Bilozir was savagely beaten under the walls of the prosecutor's office and died days later. The perpetrators have been apprehended, and an iron crown of thorns bears a sad reminder of the great loss that came to Ukrainian culture with the death of the composer. He was buried in the central alley of Lychakiv Cemetery. We end our tour of Akademichna Street near the «skyscraper» dating from the 1920s, erected in the style of so-called functionalism. It was built for countless offices and bureaus. Currently they are occupied by trade unions that are in the habit of turning a deaf ear to their members. And a sizeable part of the ground floor is occupied by a McDonald's fast-food chain outlet. Colorful packaging and pervasive advertising lure mostly kids and students. Dignified connoisseurs of good food remain true to local cuisine, where, as a local joke says, lard is always lard, and sausage is the best of fish. Traditions...

On knights, muses, and liberty on Svobody Avenue

After our promenade along Akademichna Street and back, we pass the now familiar George Hotel, Mickiewicz, and Virgin Mary until we find ourselves on Svobody Avenue (Liberty Avenue). The name of the avenue corresponds to reality. It is in fact a broad thoroughfare bustling with traffic, with a shaded parkway stretching up to the Opera House. Formerly («formerly» in Lviv can mean both a couple decades and six centuries ago) this street was known as Hetman's ramparts, and, in fact, it was one. Ramparts surrounded the walls of ancient Lviv and the Poltva was flowing in the moat circling the ramparts. To see it for yourself, keep looking to the right, as some of the ancient buildings have preserved a stronghold-like and impregnable appearance.

You will often hear this bitter joke in Lviv. The two things Lvivites always begrudge the rest of Ukraine are that Shevchenko was born in Cherkasy region and that UPA, the Ukrainian Insurgent Army, was founded in Volyn. Be that as it may, Halychans redressed this «historical injustice» with a modern commanding monument to Kobzar (Taras Shevchenko is commonly referred to as Kobzar, which is Ukrainian for bard). Although its architectural completeness is the subject of ongoing disputes, it has been erected in Lviv's very heartland which saw the revival of the national democratic movement in the late 1980s. Taras stands tall in the center of this ongoing struggle.

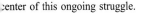

Facing Kobzar is Grand Hotel, one of Lviv's most upscale hotel and the first Ukrainian and American joint venture in our city. Ranking diplomats, business executives, foreign pop stars often stay in the hotel's suites.

To the right of the hotel, at the corner of Svobody Avenue and Hnatyuka Street there is the grand entrance to the Museum of Ethnography and Folk Art, which also houses the Institute for Ukrainian Studies. Designed by architect Zakhariyevych and decked with works of sculptor Markoni, this building had been under slow pace construction from 1874 through 1891. Built at the city's expense, the building was used as an industrial museum in which Lviv craftsmen could hone their skills using specimens on display. Later the museum stock was replenished with a sizeable collection of works of Ukrainian folk art and ethnography courtesy of the Shevchenko Scholarly Association. Currently, the museum stock and exposition feature around 80,000 relics of material and spiritual culture of the people.

A sculpture of Liberty adorns the upper part of the façade near the dome. It is one of the three sculptures known in the world, but Lviv's Liberty is the only sitting sculpture. In the early 1980s our Liberty started to claim victims, as her stone hand fell off, injuring a passerby.

Behind the Shevchenko Monument is the tree-shaded square of Ivan Pidkova enclosed in the remains of ancient walls.

In the mid-16th century, the noted Cossack chieftain got involved into Moldovan domestic strife. Cossacks captured the Moldovan capital, Yassy, and proclaimed Ivan Pidkova the Moldovan sovereign. He thus came into disfavor with Turkish Sultan Murad III who sent his great host against Pidkova. Cossacks retreated as far as Rzechpospolita where Poles apprehended Pidkova upon the Turks' request. The Polish king pledged to put him to death.

The monument was erected close to the historical site of his execution. Citizens, most of whom sympathized with Pidkova and hated Turks, were restless that day. Pidkova met his death as befits a knight. He drank to his fellow Cossacks the last cupful that one of his blood brothers handed him. Upon the executioner's request he himself set his collar straight. At the moment Pidkova's head fell to the ground, a fragment of the City Hall façade collapsed. Not to let the Polish king send the ataman's head to the sultan, Cossacks had sewn it to his decapitated body and placed it into a green coffin which Pidkova himself prepared beforehand. Later Pidkova's remains were brought to Kaniv where they were buried on the Chernecha (Monks') Hill. Later famous Cossack Yakiv Shakh, ataman Samiylo Kishka, and, two centuries and a half on, Taras Shevchenko, found their last repose on the Chernecha Hill beside Ivan Pidkova.

Having reflected on vainness and quirks of fate, we should stop to get acquainted with one more acclaimed philosopher.

Jaroslav Hasek, author of *Good Soldier Schweik*, wrote that Schweik didn't stay in Lviv too long but long enough to appreciate the good taste of Lviv bear. Our contemporaries believe that this major event happened at the site of the present Viennese Coffee Shop (Wiener Kaffeehaus). And why not... Be that as it may, now we can drink coffee or beer in the company of the bronze statue of Schweik. What does credit to the owners of the Viennese Coffee Shop is the fact that furniture and interior of the cozy outlet marvelously reproduce the ambience of the early 20th century Viennese (and Lviv) coffee shops.

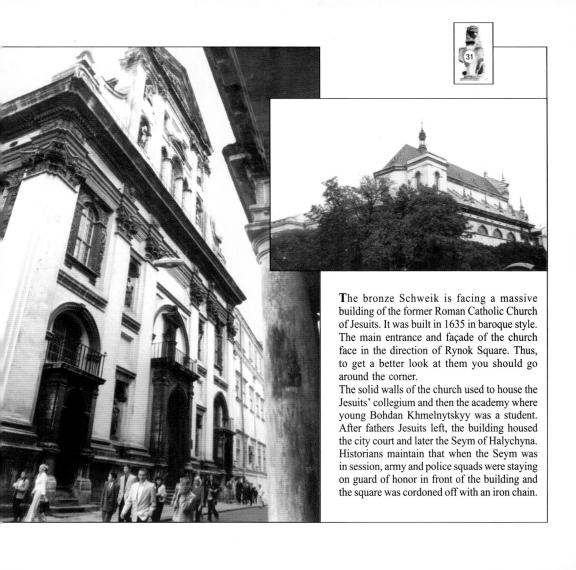

The bronze Schweik is facing a massive building of the former Roman Catholic Church of Jesuits. It was built in 1635 in baroque style. The main entrance and façade of the church face in the direction of Rynok Square. Thus, to get a better look at them you should go around the corner.

The solid walls of the church used to house the Jesuits' collegium and then the academy where young Bohdan Khmelnytskyy was a student. After fathers Jesuits left, the building housed the city court and later the Seym of Halychyna. Historians maintain that when the Seym was in session, army and police squads were staying on guard of honor in front of the building and the square was cordoned off with an iron chain.

The Academic State Opera and Ballet Theater named for Solomiya Krushelnytska is Lviv's undisputed architectural gem. Alongside the Odessa and Vienna theaters, it is considered one of the most luxurious theaters in Europe. It was designed by Sigismund Horholevskyy, a graduate of the Berlin Building Academy, in the authentic style of Viennese Renaissance. Regrettably, this proved to be the architect's first and last work, but it, nevertheless, immortalized his name. The grandeurs and completeness of the edifice are striking. The main façade is bedecked with numerous niches, columns, balustrades, cornices, and statues. Allegoric sculptures of Life and Art have been placed in the niches above the ground floor, and in the upper part above columns there are images of muses by A. Popel. The façade is crowned with bronze sculptures of Glory, Victory, and Love. The interior of the theater is even more striking. It is lavishly decorated with multicolored marble, and gilt. The main scenic curtain was painted by the outstanding representative of late academism in painting H. Semyradskyy.

Curiously, although the theater is not fitted out with powerful ventilation systems, its air is always cool and fresh. The acoustics are also splendid.

In 2000, the Lviv Opera marked its centennial, for which occasion it was thoroughly renovated. Timed to coincide with the visit of Pope John Paul II to Ukraine was a grand opera, Moses, based on the work of Ivan Franko. Unfortunately, the Pope did not attend the premier, but the production was fully and generously sponsored by the Vatican. Speaking of the money, try to find in your wallet a twenty-hryvnya note. Can you recognize the Opera on its reverse?

Another famous theater close by is even older. Now it is the National Theater named for Mariya Zankovetska. The idea to build it was put forward by a famous philanthropist, Count Stanislav Skarbek. He himself directed the construction and invited two noted Viennese architects, Pichl and Salzmann. Skarbek's theater came to be known as a theater where signers and conductors destined to become stars of world renown had given their premiers. Incidentally, Solomiya Krushelnytska herself performed here. And although the Opera House was named for her, staff and company of the Zankovetska Theatre do not bear a grudge, as they have a constellation of their own famous actors, singers, and conductors. By the way, the other day a letter was discovered in which Solomiya Krushelnytska wrote that she was not only a Ruthenian (Ukrainian), but also belonged to the world. Who would argue with that?

Opposite the main entrance to the theater, in Viche (Council) Square there is the so-called Lviv's open-air fair cum art exhibition. But first a few words about the square itself. Prior to the collapse of the Soviet Union, the democratic city fathers chose this square as a venue for various rallies and mass gatherings. But politically active Lvivites did not take to this place. Only the name remained. However, craftsmen, artists, second-hand dealers in antiques of varying value feel themselves at home here. Here you can easily buy a small keepsake to remind you of Lviv, embroidery or an authentic Hutsul plaid (inhabitants of the Carpathians are commonly referred to as Hutsuls). The atmosphere at the fair is democratic, you may and should bargain.

At the fair itself and everywhere around it there are lots of various cafes to choose and pick from. Apropos, before moving on to Rynok Square a refreshing meal might be a good idea.

«There in Lviv, in Rynok Square...»

There in Lviv in Rynok Square
News was made the other day:
«Hey, fellows, I will recruit you
And the lad got drafted,
And they gave him a saber...

A recruits' song of the time
of World War

Back in the days of Prince Lev, a colony of Germans formed near the castle which had its own elected head. When Polish King Kazimierz captured Lviv, he granted the Germans new privileges, and, before all, he permitted them to build a fortified township to the south of the Castle Hill, on the Poltva's bank. A square-shaped area, which came to be known as Rynok or Market Square, formed the center of the new town. Along its perimeter the town was surrounded with solid walls, ramparts and moats. Ramparts were named Hetman's (now Svobody Avenue), Governor's (a parkway between Pidvalna and Vynnychenka Streets), and ran along Skarbivska Street (now Lesi Ukrayinky Street) and Sobieskogo Street (now Brativ Rohatyntsiv Street). The first Town Hall was built in Rynok Square by Prince Volodyslav Opolskyy in the 1470s. It stood in flames a couple of times.

The assembly room, where the town council would assemble, was the grandest part of the old Town Hall. The council consisted of the wealthiest townspeople ('patricians'), but only Roman Catholics, Germans and Poles. The Ukrainian community of the town had been litigating with the town authorities in a bid to secure themselves equal rights. And only in 1745 the first Ukrainian (Ruthenian), Yury Kotsiy, was admitted into the council.

The old belfry towered 58 meters above the Town Hall. The Polish coat-of-arms and lion bedecked the spire of the tower. In a storm of 1672 the lion fell to the ground, which was thought to be an evil omen. Incidentally, that same year the town was besieged by Turks. Turkish cannonballs reached as far as Rynok Square.

Ever since 1404, the Town Hall tower had a clock. The one that keeps time now was made in 1851 in Vienna.

Charged with maintaining law and order, the Town Hall had its own prisons. Perpetrators of petty crimes would be jailed in a small cell above the treasury. There were real dungeons, too, known as «Dorotka», «Under the Angel», «Tatarnya». In his days, Hetman Yuriy Khmelnytskyy was held in custody there.

The City Hall acquired its modern appearance in the mid-19th century. During the revolution of 1848 which engulfed all of the Austrian Empire, Rynok Square was occupied by the Polish National Guard. The Austrian garrison was pounding them with cannonballs. The City Hall tower caught fire, its dome tumbled down together with the old clock and bells. The City Hall was rebuilt three years after the fire, but the tower did not get back its dome, and now this is 65 meter chimney is towering above the city. From this elevation tourists can marvel at the panorama of the old Lviv.

36

Let us start our tour of Rynok Square with the house at the corner of Stavropihiyska and Drukarska (Printers') Street. This is a drug store museum. Despite modern drugs on sale, the place emanates the secrets of medicine as practiced in ancient times. There is no telling whether someone was trying to discover the Philosopher's Stone here, but one of the rooms in the drugstore is covered with multicolored murals featuring the four elements of the Universe: water, fire, earth, and air. Dating from 1735, the building, which has been used as a drugstore ever since 1775, changed hands many times. One of its owners was immortalized in Lviv legends.

Mykhaylo Terletskyy, a famous philanthropist, was also an amateur card player. However, when it actually came to playing cards he was usually out of luck. But one time Terletskyy chanced to win as much as three gold coins. To celebrate this happy occurrence, the apothecary went from one coffee house and into the other, gathering his friends and spinning aphorisms about the art of card-playing. Glad to drink on the arm, his company flocked around Terletskyy. Following each of his harangues, the generous apothecary would let out a victorious sound that resembled the bleating of a goat. Word has it, since that time it has become customary to «lead the goat» in Lviv, that is, to roam in a big and noisy company from one bar to another. They say, on that day the generous apothecary Terletskyy parted with 30 gold coins.

Text to the drugstore, under No. 2 in Rynok Square there is an unmatched example of neo-baroque architecture. This ancient masonry is to this day dubbed «the house of Bandinelli». In fact, merchant Roberto Bandinelli, the son of a Florentine carver Bartolomeo Bandinelli, lived here. In 1629, he inaugurated Lviv's first regular postal service. In all probability, every Saturday more than twenty mailmen would leave this house for Zamost, Lublin, Warsaw, Gdansk, or Rzeszow, Tarnuw, Krakow...

Half a century before postmaster Bandinelli and his building appeared in Lviv, a «black masonry» (Building No. 4) of an «Italian» Petro Krassovskyy bedecked the square. In fact, Krassovskyy was a Ukrainian, and he came by his nickname for his love of Italian architecture of the Renaissance epoch, a contemporary of which he was.

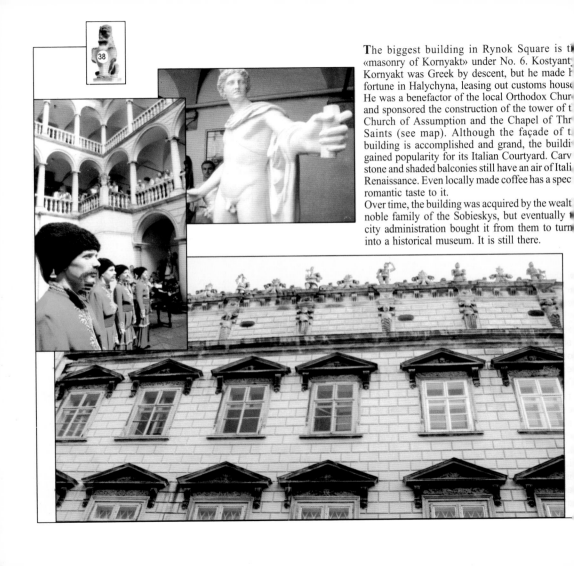

The biggest building in Rynok Square is the «masonry of Kornyakt» under No. 6. Kostyantyn Kornyakt was Greek by descent, but he made his fortune in Halychyna, leasing out customs houses. He was a benefactor of the local Orthodox Church and sponsored the construction of the tower of the Church of Assumption and the Chapel of Three Saints (see map). Although the façade of the building is accomplished and grand, the building gained popularity for its Italian Courtyard. Carved stone and shaded balconies still have an air of Italian Renaissance. Even locally made coffee has a special romantic taste to it.

Over time, the building was acquired by the wealthy noble family of the Sobieskys, but eventually the city administration bought it from them to turn it into a historical museum. It is still there.

On the south side of Rynok Square, the house No. 14 best survived the ravages of time and renovations. Built of cut stone, it preserved all the features of the initial renaissance style. Above the entrance hangs a Viennese lion with an open book dating from 1600. This used to be the dwelling place of Jan Massari, a Viennese merchant and consul.

Roughly at the same time, building No.29 was owned by the Kampian family. This family went down in history not as valorous knights or enlighteners, but as corrupt officials. First the father, Pawel Kampian, and later his son Martyn were town mayors. Forcing townspeople into debt and embezzling funds from town coffers, the Kampians became nothing short of dictators. Martyn was so barefaced as to take over from the Jesuits the big city debt and started to think that he simply bought the whole city. A year after his machination the trial, *Town community vs. Kampians* made headlines. Martyn was disgracefully dismissed as mayor, his family deprived of citizens' rights.

An unparalleled embellishment of Rynok Square are the sculptures at its corners. These are four Empi style fountains of the early 19th century featuring sculptures of Greek and Roman gods, Neptune, Dian Adonis, and Amphitrite. The four of them, the work of a gifted artist Vitver, were built in the square tw centuries ago.

inally, just have a look under
our feet. Relayed dozens of
mes, these cobblestones with
qual indifference and patience
d been eating away at the soles
kings and paupers, wise men
d fools, great philanthropists
d thieves. Their faces fade in the
rkness of time, but even from
is mind-boggling distance you
n hear their voices imprinted on
e age-old stones. The voices of
vites... Can you hear them?

First Armenians settled in Lviv almost at the time it was founded, i the second half of the 13th century. Danylo Halytskyy himself invite Armenian craftsmen, who had been known for their superior skill Initially, Armenians settled densely at the foot of the Castle Hill, no Pidzamcha Street. After Lviv had been captured by Kazimierz III, som Armenians settled in the so-called Low Castle (contrasted with the Cast Hill, often referred to as the High Castle). That's where Ormiansk (Virmenska) Street (derived from Polish «Ormianie» for Armenian emerged. However, the Armenians were known not only for the craftsmanship. Caucasian merchants played an important role in trad contacts with the countries of the East. Their caravans traveled as far Cairo, Istanbul, and Baghdad. Goods from the East on Lviv marke were traditionally called Armenian and thus were valued highl According to foreign merchants, as early as in the 15th century, Armeni Street, Rynok Square, and Ruthenian (Ruska) Street were cobbled, the architecture and sanitation cutting-edge. Water supply and drai sewerage were customary for residents of this district.

In 1527, a fire broke out in a brewery in the street next to Armenian. Fire spread onto Armenian Street and then over the entire town. This fire wiped out gems of Lviv's Gothic architecture.

The center of the colony's life was the Armenian Cathedral. The architectural ensemble comprises the church itself, the premises of the former nunnery, and the Palace of Armenian Archbishops. This is, by all accounts, the oldest intact edifice in Lviv which is a unique example of Armenian architecture. Solid 140-centimeter walls built of cut stone had been covered with stone slabs on the inside and outside. Some fragments dating five centuries back have lasted to this day. The structure of the dome is unique. It rests on hollow ribs made of earthenware jugs. On the whole, the cathedral has undergone a lot of changes as a result of renovations in the wake of numerous fires.

In January 2001, divine services resumed in the cathedral after a lengthy pause. Word has it, this was due to the Pope's visit to Lviv. In fact, the Pope did visit the renewed premises of the cathedral.

Spiritual life, however, always comes hand in hand with secular pleasures. At one time, a decade or two ago a coffee shop, In Virmenska, was a favorite venue for Lviv's nonconformists. A special atmosphere of olden times and modern lack of constraint, plus really delicious Turkish coffee made this place a crowd puller. There was not enough room in the coffee shop and habitués would squat right in the street. Something of the spirit of those days is still lingering in the air.

Fanciers of authentic Armenian cognac can indulge in it in the Ararat coffee shop.

Lviv's creative Bohemia is now quartered at the very end of Armenian Street, in the building of the association of artists, Dzyha (Whirligig). That's where avant-garde mixes with retro, especially in the extravagant coffee shop of the Whirligig.

The very end of Armenian Street opens on a square in front of the Monastery of the Dominicans. According to legend, Prince Lev built his manor at this site. In the late 13th century, his wife Constance invited fathers Dominicans to Lviv. At first, a small wooden monastery was built for them, and in 1405 — a Roman-Catholic Church of the God's Body. Three years from then the church burnt down. Assiduous Dominicans gradually rebuilt it, using stone and brick, in the Gothic style. The heartrending tale of Halshka Ostrozka is connected with this church.

After her famous father met his quietus, Princess Ostrozka came into a fortune. It was only natural that there instantly appeared numerous suitors eager to lay their hands on the estate of the Ostrozkyys. The girl was not really into marriage, but she was forced into marriage with Polish tycoon, Lukasz Gurka. Halshka's mother, Beata revolted against this abuse of her daughter. Aided by the king's mother, the

two of them escaped to Lviv and requested protection from the Dominicans. Disguised as an old monk, Prince Simeon Slutskyy, beloved by the daughter and mother Ostrozkyys, stole into the monastery where they secretly married.

Lukasz Gurka, exasperated by this escapade surrounded the monastery. Having shut off water supply to the monastery, he forced the escapees to give themselves up. Hapless Halshka Ostrozka was imprisoned in the High Castle pending the king's decision. The king gave Ostrozka back to Gurka. But the proud princess never recognized Lukasz as her legitimate husband. Thwarted morally, she died years later in the Polish castle of Szamotuly. To this day, locals point to the tower of the «black princess» dubbed so because until her last day she wore black apparel.

In 1707, in the refectory of the Dominicans' monastery Russian Czar Peter I signed the agreement with Polish nobles on the joint war on the Swedes.

In the mid-18th century, the old church was torn down to be replaced by a new one in Baroque style. Its façade was adorned with the Dominicans' coat-of-arms featuring a dog lying on a book and holding a torch in his mouth. «Domini canes» is Latin for the «Dogs of God». According to legend, the mother of Domingo de Guzman, founder of the Order, dreamt of an angel who told her that she would give birth to a torch, which would set fire to enemies of the holy faith. The book is a symbol of the Holy Writ.

Currently the monastery is housing the museums of history of religion. The cathedral has been given over to worshipers. Divine services are sometimes celebrated to the accompaniment of organ music. The cathedral has one of the three working organs in Lviv.

From Rynok Square you can take Serbska (Serb) Street to Staroyevreyska (Old Jewish) Street. As the latter's name suggests, this street was inhabited by the Jewish community of Lviv. Under constant pressure from the Christian majority, Jews were, nonetheless, actively doing their business in Lviv. They would lend money with interest as well as in exchange for pawned property, traded in goods from overseas and wines. The exclusive business of Jews was running illegal and half-legal brothels. One of the last of them was in the building at the corner of Serbian and Ruthenian Streets, now housing Bank Lviv. In Staroyevreyska Street, remains of the groundwork of an ancient synagogue, Golden Rose, have lasted to this day. According to legend, a certain Jew Nakhmanovich, who sponsored the construction, sacrificed the chastity of his daughter, Rosa, to obtain a permit to build the synagogue. Though another legend says that Rosa offered herself to some ranking official to obtain the permit and took her life afterwards.

Another ploy is connected with the construction of the synagogue. City fathers imposed a limitation on the height of the Judaic temple so that it would not outshine Christian churches. Then inventive Jews built the floor a couple meters below ground level. In 1942 a Nazi occupation troops blew up Golden Rose. And with such precision that none of the surrounding buildings was damaged. Lviv's Jewish community hopes to rebuild the synagogue.

The name of Ruthenian Street does not mean that Ruthenian Ukrainians lived only there in Lviv. This block has always been a center of Ruthenian culture and Orthodoxy. Even at times when repressions of Catholics and Polish authorities were especially fierce. Building No. 20 in Ruthenian Street is especially interesting in this respect. Built for a Ukrainian insurance company, Dniester, in the early 20th century in secession style and richly decorated with ceramics and folk ornaments, it had a theater hall where the premiere of *Stolen Happiness*, a popular play by Ivan Franko was staged in 1907. A year later, a famous Ukrainian actor and director, Les Kurbas made his debut, playing the leading part in a play called *Jews*. This building also housed a students' sports association, Ukraine. The association sired Ukraine's first ice hockey team, Ukraine, and its goalkeeper, M. Skrypiy, a.k.a. Tiger, was the first in the world to wear a protective face mask. The goalkeeper made it from an old helmet and a mesh. Currently building No. 20 houses an outpatients' clinic and gym.

The architectural ensemble of the Church of Assumption is a real gem of Ukrainian Renaissance. The church used to be patronized by the Stauropegian Society which, as has been mentioned, opposed the Catholic and Polish expansion and fought for the civil rights of the Ruthenians. Amazingly, the fight for equal rights of Ukrainian citizens with other townspeople lasted a hundred and forty (!) years. And only in 1745 were Ukrainians admitted into artisans' guilds and bodies of self-government.

The church ran a library, school, museum, and print shop. In 1918, the first assembly of the Ukrainian National Council was held here, which later turned into the Parliament of the West Ukrainian People's Republic. Under the Council's decree, on November 1, 1918 the national blue-and-yellow flag was for the first time hoisted by strilets Stepan Pankivskyy on the City Hall spire.

As in olden times, the church ensemble comprise the church itself, tower (belfry) of Kornyakt, an chapel of the Three Saints. The church dates from th mid-16th century. It stood in flames a couple of times, b each time was rebuilt mostly by the Stauropegian Society The construction and periodical renovations of the churc was sponsored by Moldavian princes, Zaporozhzhia Hetman Petro Konashevych-Sahaydachnyy, and eve Russian Czar Fedor Ivanovich.

The 66 meters high tower adjoining the church i considered the most beautiful belfry in Lviv. Amon its bells is Lviv's biggest bell, Kyrylo. Two meters i diameter, it weighs four tones. The resounding don of Kyrylo has long been an object of envy of Catholi priesthood. In 1594-1595, the Stauropegian Societ was contesting at law the right to sound the bell at th top of its voice.

In 1779, a misfortune befell the bell. During downpour, the lightning hit the tower. Electricit charge was so big that part of the belfry burnt dow and the bell melted. Four years later Kyrylo was ca anew (Ukrainian master F. Polyanskyy) and to thi day it resounds above Lviv from where, by a accounts, Leopolis started…

In fact, Halychyna and Volyn Prince and King Danyl would build castles-fortresses across the borderland of his principality. One of them he named for his so Historians traditionally date Lviv's age from 125 when Leopolis was first mentioned in the Halychyn and Volyn Chronicle. However, the other day whe tram lines were being replaced in Ruthenian Stree builders, and later archaeologists, discovered th remains of a tower dating from before 1256. Unlik women, our city would not mind taking on a coupl more years.

n the square in front of the Church of Assumption, there s the grand monument to Ivan Fedorov, a.k.a. Fedorovych r Muscovite. The monument was unveiled in 1975. And lthough historians keep arguing whether the Muscovite s in fact the first printer, he is no doubt the first Ruthenian rinter. Persecuted by boyars in Moscow, Fedorov (allegedly f Belorussian descent) found sponsors and aides precisely mong Lviv's Ruthenians. In all probability, here (in the hurch of St. Onufriy, in Bohdan Khmelnytskyy Street) e first book in the Ukrainian land, *The Apostle*, came ff the presses. Here, again, he found his last repose.

he work of Fedorov is continued by teachers and students f the Ukrainian Academy of Printing. One of its buildings here, in Pidvalna (Rampart Frontage) Street.

ehind the old ramparts above Pidvalna Street and hidden nder the canopy of chestnuts are the solid walls of the unpowder Tower. But let us leave it, as well as the High astle, for later. Let us go down now familiar Ruthenian treet and cross Rynok Square to Cathedral Square.

Gothic, Turkish cannonballs, and human ambition

The Bishop's Cathedral is considered the only classical example of sacral Gothic in Lviv. But, be honest, this cathedral is the only one which added to its basic architectural style virtually a of the styles known later. The mater is that, laid in the second half of the 14th century, the cathedral was built and rebuilt during 140 years. During this time the building acquired elemen of rococo, Baroque, Renaissance. And although it was reconstructed even later, one can say th the cathedral acquired its main features in the late 18th century. Then the main tower was raise to 64 meters and rounded off with an original baroque dome.

At one time, the cathedral was in the midst of the so-calle interconfessional confrontations. In 1629, Uniate bishops celebrate divine service there. This angered the citizens, most of whom we Orthodox. These events marked the start of the strife, which is a so spot for Halychans.

Until the late 18th century, the patch in front of the cathedral w occupied by the Catholic graveyard. Not to worry, you do not tread th remains of your forefathers. Upon the order of the Austrian Emper the graveyard was carefully relocated to the outskirts of the town.

As a reminder of the siege of Lviv by the Turks and Cossacks of Pet Doroshenko, three cannonballs had been hanged on the wall of the cathedr

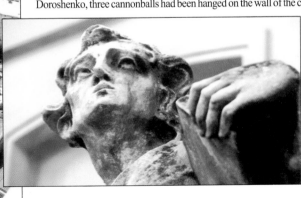

Roman Catholics have preserved a similar reminder of the siege of the town by the Ukrainian Halytska Army in 1918.

Around the cathedral, a number of chapels, mostly familial, have remained intact. The Kampians and Boims Chapels deserve special mention.

The Boims Chapel is decorated with carvings in white stone featuring the history of life of Jesus Christ. The artists used their contemporaries as models, thus we can see in them an assembled image of a 17th century Lvivite. The chapel is crowned with a dome with a sculpture of Christ in the Gethsemane. The sculpture is indeed unique. The Kampian family decorated their chapel on the outside with carved marble slabs also featuring themes from the Gospel. A faded fresco featuring the Mother of God with Jesus adorns the eastern side of the chapel. Inside the chapel there are busts of Pawel and Martyn Kampians.

Historians are in some doubt as to when the chapels were built. However, it is known that they were being built at roughly the same time when the town witnessed an ambitious confrontation between the two influential families. Their representatives took turns as town mayors, constantly pestering one another.

If Georgij Boim first earned public recognition, having struck a fortune dealing in wines from overseas, and then was elected mayor, then we have already mentioned the deeds of the Kampian family. Corrupt to their backbone, the two of them made a fast buck, blatantly abusing their position. For this they paid dearly, defamed and stripped of citizens' rights.

Be that as it may, the strife between the two families on an ego trip left Lviv residents these inimitable monuments of architecture. Everything is transient, only music is eternal. A reminder of this simple truth is an organ which has been for 160 years resonating in the Cathedral. Amen...

51

Bernardinian's trace, Arsenal Museum

The former Church and Monastery of the Bernardinians (a hundred and fifty steps down Serbian Street from Rynok Square) are another example of a successful combination of a number of architectural styles. They were built in the 17th century first by builder Pavlo Rymlyanyn and, after he died, by Ambroziy Prykhylnyy. The difference in styles can be attributed to the different tastes of the architects. At that time, the monastery served as a defense outpost of Lviv, thus it had massive fortifications. The defensive wall and the Hlynyanska tower have lasted to this day. The tower of the church itself is 38 meters high with a restored tower clock dating from the 18th century. The monastery itself and its inhabitants are the subject of countless legends, though not always pious and ascetic just like the ways of brothers Bernardinians.

In the courtyard of the monastery there is a rotunda well, built in 1720. The vault of the rotunda features a fresco dedicated to the life and miracle of St. Jan from Duklya. This saint was a Bernardinian monk who died in 1484. A year after his death, a well sprung up from the monk's grave. Then, during the siege of Lviv of 1648, Saint Jan appeared in the sky and shielded the town from bullets.

Without a doubt, brothers Bernardinians celebrated this miracle in a proper way because they knew something about secular joys, namely wine, beer, good food, and just name it... But later about this.

The Bernardinian well had also been through tragic times. According to legend, brothers monks dumped into it the bodies of treacherously slain townspeople who attempted to open the town gates for the host of Bohdan Khmelnytskyy. However, according to another legend, the monks themselves had been dropped there by Cossacks. A different legend has it unfaithful women had been dumped into it.

When renovating the monastery, builders discovered an underground passage leading in the direction of the Nunnery of Clarites which used to stand in front of the Bernardinian cloister in Mytna (Customs) Square. Underground vaults of the Bernardinians still guard their secrets. During German occupation, Jewish families took shelter in there.

Currently, the former Roman Catholic Church of the Bernardinians houses the Greek Catholic Church of St. Andrew. Part of the church premises is occupied by the Central Historical Archives in Lviv, one of the richest in Europe.

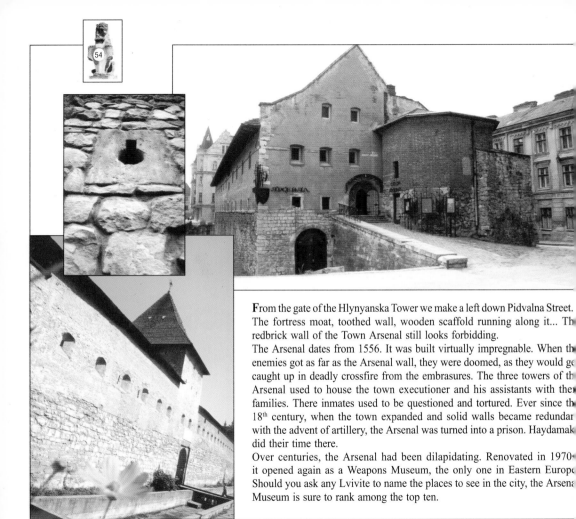

From the gate of the Hlynyanska Tower we make a left down Pidvalna Street. The fortress moat, toothed wall, wooden scaffold running along it... The redbrick wall of the Town Arsenal still looks forbidding.

The Arsenal dates from 1556. It was built virtually impregnable. When the enemies got as far as the Arsenal wall, they were doomed, as they would get caught up in deadly crossfire from the embrasures. The three towers of the Arsenal used to house the town executioner and his assistants with their families. There inmates used to be questioned and tortured. Ever since the 18th century, when the town expanded and solid walls became redundant with the advent of artillery, the Arsenal was turned into a prison. Haydamaks did their time there.

Over centuries, the Arsenal had been dilapidating. Renovated in 1970s, it opened again as a Weapons Museum, the only one in Eastern Europe. Should you ask any Lvivite to name the places to see in the city, the Arsenal Museum is sure to rank among the top ten.

special feature of Pidvalna Street is the metallic grating sound of
ams running to and fro. At one time the first horse-drawn tram rattled
own this street, and before long an electric tram replaced it. Ever
nce, you would often hear a popular song:

> *Trams chase trams,*
> *And another one follows them,*
> *And behind that tram*
> *Yet another tram...*

his song is about Pidvalna Street.

ccording to original designs, the tracks were to be straight and pass
ght under the windows of the governor's palace (now the Regional
blast State Administration). But the then governor, Badeni, freaked
at the thought of «an iron tram grating under his very nose».
rightened builders could not but turn the tracks down Pidvalna Street.
s a result, instead of one, now there are three sharp turns of the lines.
hey are still there, so as to remind Lvivites that the governor's peace is
bove all. Governors come and go, but the ways of power stay unchanged.

Gunpowder Tower, democracy, and lions

We have returned to the square in front of the Church of Assumption deliberatel so that we could see the Gunpowder Tower on our way to the Castle Hill.

The name of the ancient fortification is not misleading. That's where gunpowd was stored. However, in peacetime it served as a makeshift granary not to put th city at risk of a sudden explosion.

From the embrasures of the Gunpowder Tower the abovementioned Poli tycoon Gurka fired at the Dominicans' Monastery, where young Prince Ostrozka took shelter. From here, a descendant of the Ubaldini family in 16 fired a shot at Bohdan Khmelnytskyy. Luckily, the bullet fell under the hoo of the Hetman's horse.

The tower was used as a makeshift granary until the late 1950s, when it becam the House of Architects.

The Gunpowder Tower has also left a mark on modern history. The first assemb of the People's Movement of Ukraine was held here. With the building of th Regional Committee of the then ruling Communist Party (now the Regional Sta Administration building) within reach, national democratic forces, which ouste the Communists shortly afterwards, held their meetings here.

You can walk past the lions irresponsibly sleeping while being on guard into th tower to have a cup of coffee with Lviv artists in a cozy coffee shop.

Incidentally, the theme of lions is very popular and respected in our city. Ancient and modern, sleepy and vigilant, stone and metal, they are omnipresent. Proud and strong, they are never aggressive and do not attack passersby. Perhaps, true Lvivites take after them in their ways.

One such lion, arguably the oldest, contemplates the city from the Castle Hill where we are headed.

On the Castle Hill

It is easier to ascend the Castle Hill from the side of the Gunpowder Tower, across the uneven cobbled Lysenka Street, past the Monument to Prosvita (Enlightenment), up Hutsulska and Opryshkivska Streets. Incidentally, Hutsulska Street named so in the honor of Carpathian highlanders who fought bravely against Polish and Lithuanian invaders in the 14th century. Farther up is an old street bearing the historic name of Maksym Kryvonis. Under his command, the High Castle was captured, although in those times its walls were considered impregnable.

ith the advance of artillery, the walls and towers of the castle became redundant.
e Austrian authorities permitted the townspeople to dismantle the castle walls,
th stones to be used in households, which they did successfully. There are scattered
mains of the foundations and paths... Only a fragment of the castle wall at the
othill has remained intact.

owever, three centuries since the singing of the Union of Lublin the Austrian
thorities, cautious of national sentiments, with unexpected ease permitted the Poles
raise a symbolic burial mound on the Castle Hill. It took thirty one (!) years to
ise it, from 1869 to 1900. However, with no fundamental calculations performed,
fore long part of the mound came tumbling down. The remains of that mound are
w the observation platform on the hill.

ow it is impossible to see from the hill what princes, commandants, or sentinels on
e castle walls once saw. And not only because the city has grown and changed
yond recognition. Ever since 1835, the Castle Hill was methodically planted with
es which have grown to form an ancient park. Under overhanging trees, lovers
iddle in a quiet nook, elderly Lvivites stroll with their grandchildren, tourists marvel
the beauty of the opening vistas of the city which survived the ravages of time and
s been preserved for the generations to come.

emember Lviv like this. Now it is yours, too...

If you consider yourself a real lover of antiqu\[e\] you should spend a whole day visiting the Lvi\[v\] museums. And it's not only for the reason th\[at\] mysteries and spirit of the past require slo\[w\] walking and slow flow of thoughts. Official\[ly\] there are over thirty museums in Lviv, b\[ut\] churches, exhibition halls, galleries, monumer\[ts\] should be added to this number…

We are going to tell you about four of the\[m\] which will give you an idea of the immen\[se\] treasures, carefully kept by the Lvivites for t\[he\] coming generations.

Smiling «Castles» of Halychans

Descending from Castle Hill down to Lychakivska Street and keeping on going along (asking always-friendly locals the way) Krupyarska, Striletska and Chernecha Hora Streets, you will finally get to Shevchenkivskyy Hay (*Grove*). This place has been long known as Kaiserwald. The hills, like everything in Lviv, once were the stage for historic dramas and comedies (therefore the life itself — according to Shakespeare).

The Lion's Hill, named so, most probably, in honour of Prince Lev, was later renamed into Piskova (*Sand*) Hill, because stone and sand was extracted from its slopes. There is also a story about the man who once was walking on this hill. It was snowing heavily, wind bent the trees down. Suddenly there rose a column of sand transforming into the image of motionless knight in full armor. This is how the legend of the guarding knight was born.

Many years ago people's vineyards and gardens would grow on the slopes of the hills. Lviv used to make its own wine! Once this place was visited by the Kaiser Joseph II. To commemorate this epochal event, the stature of Minerva was erected here, which was for some reason destroyed in the early 20th century. And ever since the Kaiser's visit the hill covered with wood has been called Kaiserwald (*the Kaiser's Wood*).

Kaiserwald also pertains to Modern Ukrainian history. It was the place, where a national army was organized and where Sichovi Striltsi regiments exercised in shooting and scouting. It soon proved useful to them in the trenches of the World War I and in the battle-fields of occupied Ukrainian lands.

Today Kaiserwald — Shevchenkivskyy Hay is one of the favorite places for Lvivites to spend their leisure. Every year before Easter the people of Lviv, especially the youth, undertake cleaning and organizing of this area. And the Field of Songs is often the venue of important artistic events.

But the main attraction of the grove is the Museum of Folk Architecture and Lifestyle naturally integrated into the landscape. Walking along the paths, trodden out by the feet of thousands of tourists, we find ourselves in the Pre-Carpathian village of the 19th century. Or, perhaps the 17th ... A couple of centuries do not make much difference for ancient and wise traditions of folk wooden architecture, don't they? It's something to learn for us, the children of concrete, asphalt and glass.

It was in our time that by the efforts of scholars timber houses and churches, typical for this area, were found in far and near villages of Halychyna, renovated and carefully moved to the grove. The British say: «My home is my castle». Ukrainian timber «castles» breath with the warmth of natural wood, hospitality and kindness. The spirit of their dwellers still lives here.

Here, in the shade of age-old trees, is a good place to think of eternity and our mission on the earth, because everyone's path always ends (although better later than sooner) amidst solemn silence of a cemetery. Like in Lychakiv ...

61

Lviv necropolis

On the way to Lychakiv Cemetery you cannot miss St. Peter and Paul's Church. According to chroniclers of that time, it was built as a road chapel so that travelers and merchants could say their prayers for a successful journey. Unfortunately, not all of them were fortunate to come back home – this road, called Hlynyanskyy Tract, led to Turkey and Moskovia and was not very safe.

After saying a quiet prayer having passed the so-called Mars's Field we are approaching the gate of Lychakiv Cemetery. It dates back to the 16th century, but at that time it was not half that (please forgive this word) prestigious as today. It was mostly the place for those who died of plague or other contagious diseases. At that time each church had an adjoining cemetery. But in the late 18th century by the Kaiser's decree these churches had to be moved outside the city, therefore several suburb areas were allocated for this purpose.

One of such areas was vacant land near the village of Lychakiv, which was later integrated into the city. The oldest part of the original cemetery is on the top of the hill, near the pavilion. The gravestones and chapels date back to the late 18th century.

With time, the city authorities decided that the most celebrated Lvivites are to be buried in Lychakiv Cemetery. It became the resting place for Solomiya Krushelnytska, Ivan Franko, Mykhaylo Pavlyk, Markiyan Shashkevych, Anatoliy Vakhnyanyn, Pavlyn Svyentsitskyy, Volodymyr Barvinskyy, Stanislav Lyudkevych, Ivan Verkhratskyy, Hryhoriy Tyutyunnyk ... You can come across some of these famous names in our guide, others also did contribute much to Ukrainian culture and science. As a whole, there are over three thousand gravestones and chapels. Many of them are genuine masterpieces. Among our prominent contemporaries, who found their resting place in Lviv necropolis are Volodymyr Ivasyuk and Ihor Bilozir. Today burials in the central area of the cemetery are allowed only in exceptional cases and only for very famous people.

Rest in peace...

Here ... the cosmonauts spoke with God

We are already familiar with Dominicans' Cathedral. But there is one more thing about it, which is worth attention. During the atheistic boom in the Soviet time, in 1970, a part of the cathedral buildings was transformed into the museum of these aggressive studies. Under the shield of «unveiling» the «opium for people», the scholars managed to save beautiful examples of religious items: icons, sculptures, printed issues. Thanks to them now we have the Museum of Religion, which is probably unique in Ukraine.

The whole ensemble of the cathedral and monastery is full of mysteries and legends. The icon of Rus' Holy Virgin the Victoria has always been the holy protector of the cathedral (today the copy of the 18th century can be seen in the altar). They say, the original icon of the 10th century was brought from Byzantium to Kyiv by the Prince Volodymyr's wife Anna. Maybe, it was the protection of the Holy Virgin, which was sought here by the princess Ostrozka, hiding from the unloved man. Do you remember?

Some people say, that in the corridors and basements of the monastery the ghosts can still be encountered. In the beginning of the last century the cathedral was associated with the black knight. His shadow appears each night in black hat and cloak. Maybe, it was the nobleman, the beloved of Halshka Ostrozka, who could not share his love with her? In any case, the unique energy and vibroacoustics of the Dominicans' Ensemble are much spoken about …

In different times the monastery was visited by people, whose fates were tragically bound together. Those were Russian Czar Peter I, Swedish King Charles XII and Ukrainian Hetman Mazepa. The altar is the heart of the cathedral-museum. It is embellished with exquisite wooden sculptures by the famous sculptor of the 18th century Maciej Polejowski. The sculptures of saints which surround the cathedral above the galleries are very impressive, too. They capture the eye and invite us to leave the everyday life behind and send our prayers and thoughts to the Almighty.

Back in the time, when the Museum of Religion was still the Museum of Atheism, one instructive anecdote appeared and spread. One of the Soviet cosmonauts was invited to the Museum for the meeting with schoolchildren. One curious boy asked the cosmonaut if he didn't happen to see God behind the clouds. The cosmonaut was silent for a while and finally answered in a low voice: «I thank God for coming back to the Earth». Everyone is under the God... All is vanity...

This idea is expressed by the charming tunes of the cathedral organ of the 17th century. Badly damaged in the Soviet times, it was then restored in 1985 to inspire the people's souls. The instrument is not very big, but it is pretty the same as those which were played by Bach, Händel, Buxtehude or Couperin ... Have a look at the posters, maybe you are lucky to visit the concert of organ and chamber music under the vaults of Dominicans' Cathedral.

65

The spirit of Bonaparte must be here

After a long journey we come back to Rynok Square. It is a special museum in th open air, a unique combination of epochs and styles. The adornment of the square the History Museum with the richest collection in the city.

According to one of the versions, it was founded in 1893. It now contains over 33 thousand of exhibits. Some of them are rarities of world significance. Among ther are old books of the 12th — 17th centuries, the earliest representation of Lviv and it coats of arms (see picture), Turkish military tents of the 17th century, the saddle o Ottoman vizier Kara-Mustafa, taken as a trophy in the battle of Vienna of 1683 armors of winged hussars and Hutsuls' (Carpathian highlanders') weapon, ancier orders of many countries of Europe and Asia, decorated with precious stones an colored enamel.

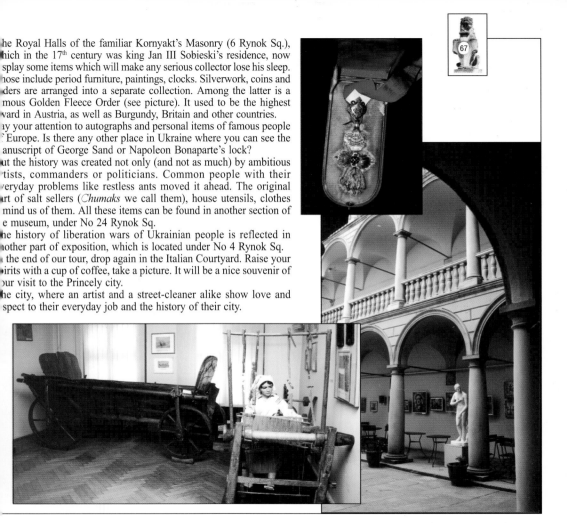

he Royal Halls of the familiar Kornyakt's Masonry (6 Rynok Sq.), hich in the 17th century was king Jan III Sobieski's residence, now splay some items which will make any serious collector lose his sleep. hose include period furniture, paintings, clocks. Silverwork, coins and ders are arranged into a separate collection. Among the latter is a mous Golden Fleece Order (see picture). It used to be the highest ward in Austria, as well as Burgundy, Britain and other countries.

ay your attention to autographs and personal items of famous people Europe. Is there any other place in Ukraine where you can see the anuscript of George Sand or Napoleon Bonaparte's lock?

ut the history was created not only (and not as much) by ambitious tists, commanders or politicians. Common people with their veryday problems like restless ants moved it ahead. The original rt of salt sellers (*Chumaks* we call them), house utensils, clothes mind us of them. All these items can be found in another section of e museum, under No 24 Rynok Sq.

he history of liberation wars of Ukrainian people is reflected in other part of exposition, which is located under No 4 Rynok Sq.

the end of our tour, drop again in the Italian Courtyard. Raise your irits with a cup of coffee, take a picture. It will be a nice souvenir of our visit to the Princely city.

he city, where an artist and a street-cleaner alike show love and spect to their everyday job and the history of their city.

67

Public transportation, taxis

The public transportation network in Lviv is quite developed and multifarious. Electric transport is municipally owned. It loss-making, and thus it is rather dilapidated and is an eyesore. Nonetheless, it is the cheapest means of transportation, wi privileges granted to the disabled, students, underage children, and veterans of all the wars.

There are nine tram routes in the city. Most of them had been laid before World War II. That is why the trams run crosstov to where there used to be city outskirts.

The trolleybus network developed in the second half of the 20th century to cater to the needs of inhabitants of new fast-growi districts. A dozen routes are served by roughly a hundred trolleybuses of Czech or Lviv makes.

Both trolleybus and tram fares cost the same, UAH 0.50 per person, the distance to be traveled notwithstanding. Fares a collected by conductors. You should not be looking for them, as they will find you themselves. You are also expected to p for your cumbersome luggage, but, in fact, nobody does it or insists that you do it.

The past couple of years have seen an unprecedented and almost chaotic growth of a commercial kind of public transportatic the so-called «route minibuses». Everything started in a quite civilized manner with Peugeot minibuses. These compact bus seemed to have provided a solution to the eternal problem of public transportation in cramped Lviv streets. However, befc long these cheap Turkish-made buses started to break down and lose their appeal and comfort in fully packed passeng compartments. That's when hundreds of makeshift passenger busses, slapdash remakes from Mercedes, DAF minivans, a God-knows-what else, engulfed the city. These buses lack comfortable seats and ventilation. Shuttling hundreds of thousan

of commuters from the suburbs to the downtown a back, they have made city traffic extremely diffic and often even dangerous. Only now the city fathe set about regulating this traffic in a bid to protect t rights of passengers.

A fare in the minibus costs UAH 0.80. The money collected by the driver while the bus is on the mov And don't you expect to get a receipt.

A taxi ride will prove a more comfortable, fast and safer way to get to your destination.

The majority of outdated VAZ or GAZ taxis (former two most popular makes of passenger cars) roami the city in search of passengers have been long cryi out to be dumped. Their drivers only pretend to wc for some taxi companies and thus they cann guarantee you a smooth ride.

round two dozen radio taxi services have been registered, but most of them
e a handpicked team which often play according to their own rules and without
coach. When you call a taxi, the dispatcher will not tell you whether a relatively
w foreign-made car or soiled and beat-up old jalopy will come to pick you
. Though the fare will cost you as much.

lly legal, licensed, and topnotch are only a few taxi services in Lviv. You can
e a receptionist's phone in a restaurant or hotel, or even you mobile phone to
ll the radio taxi service. Just give the dispatcher the address and number of
e phone you are calling from. The dispatcher will call you as soon as the taxi
rives, which will normally take 15 minutes or 20 to 25 minutes during the rush hour.

he fare within the city limits may vary from UAH 8 to 20. Should you need to hire a taxi for a little longer, you should
gotiate the price with the driver at around UAH 15—20 per hour. Your driver may also prove to be a quite passable guide.
hat's more, he won't charge you any extras for his services.

u can as well call a taxi to pick you up from suburban motels or restaurants. This will cost you an additional UAH 7–8.

he drivers of the Radar-Service radio taxi company, which you can call at 000, are arguably Lviv's best trained. Their bright
d Nubiras or Lanoses, manufactured at a Ukrainian and Korean joint venture, are decorated with yellow checkerboard
tterns, equipped with two-way radios, and (the only in Lviv) with electronic fare meters. The fare meter prints out a receipt
dicating the amount to be paid, the distance traveled, date and time.

ps for drivers of such taxis do not normally exceed 10 percent of the fare. The other drivers, not counting on your generosity,
ll add them to the fare themselves.

Hotels, restaurants, bars

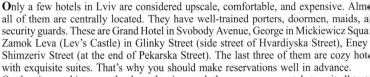

Only a few hotels in Lviv are considered upscale, comfortable, and expensive. Almost all of them are centrally located. They have well-trained porters, doormen, maids, and security guards. These are Grand Hotel in Svobody Avenue, George in Mickiewicz Square, Zamok Leva (Lev's Castle) in Glinky Street (side street of Hvardiyska Street), Eney in Shimzeriv Street (at the end of Pekarska Street). The last three of them are cozy hotels with exquisite suites. That's why you should make reservations well in advance.

On the city outskirts, mostly along the ring road, there are many motels to suit all tastes. In the green suburban settlement of Bryukhovychi, Motel Olena with a restaurant, sauna and parking lot, gets our nod.

There are more than enough middleclass hotels, but it does not mean that they lack good service, many-bedroom luxury suites, bars, restaurants, and trained servants. The price of a one-bedroom suite per person per night there is UAH 100 or thereabouts. Among them are Dniester in 6 Mateyka Street (above the Ivan Franko Park), NTON in Shevchenko Street, Suputnyk in 116 Knyahyni Olhy Street, Tustan near the airport, Hetman in Volodymyra Velykoho Street.

For unpretentious guests there are «starless» hotels in which the price per person per night will not exceed UAH 50. They also have restaurants, bars, telephones, but... Let's face it, they are a far cry from Hilton. Among them are Lviv Hotel in Chornovola Avenue (a minute's walk from the city center), Tourist at 103 Konovaltsya Street, Karpaty at the end of Kleparivska Street, near the brewery.

Telephone numbers of hotel administrators

Grand Hotel	....	72-12-22
George	....	72-59-52
Eney	....	76-87-99
Zamok Leva	....	35-11-00
Dniester	....	72-07-83
Tustan	....	69-28-82
Suputnyk	....	64-58-22
NTON	....	33-31-23
Lviv	....	79-22-70
Karpaty	....	33-34-27
Olena Motel	....	59-51-81

the city outskirts, mostly along the ring road, there are quite a few motels
h restaurants, parking lots, and saunas, to suite all tastes and pockets.
ere is hardly any other town in Ukraine which has as many various restaurants,
eries, cafes, coffee shops, pizzerias. To mention and describe at least the most
pular of them, we would have to compile a separate guidebook. Thus, counting
our own taste and experience, we will mention but a few of them.
st like hotels they are grouped according to the price, interior design, quality of
vice and food.
e top quality label can be attached to restaurants where a full-value lunch for
person can cost UAH 50—100.

agara Restaurant has recently opened in Svobody Avenue, opposite Virgin
ry. Massive wooden furniture, quietness, a sizeable menu of European and
ional dishes to pick and chose from. In Rynok Square, one of the vaults houses
unmatched café, Zoloty Vepr (Golden Wild Boar). There everything is fashioned
the Middle Ages style. Only service and kitchen appliances are modern. By all
counts, Ukrainian dishes taste better in the countryside or in an essentially
rpathian interior. For an unparalleled experience go to restaurant Kolyba
radle), five kilometers from Lviv in Bryukhovychi. It was refurbished especially
heads of European states that came to Lviv for the summit of presidents.

upscale restaurants tables are not normally reserved in advance, as they are never crowded.

iv cafes offer menus you would normally find in small eateries. There you will invariably find pizza, deruny (potato
ncakes), fried chicken, steak, and salad. The prices, however, are twice as low as in Lviv's upscale restaurants and much
ver than, say, in Kyiv cafes. By contrast, the atmosphere here is more democratic. Cafes At Giovanni's at the corner of
efanyka and Chaykovskoho Streets, Chervona Kalyna (Red Cranberry) at the corner of Chaykovskoho and Kovzhuna
eet, Knyazhyy Kelykh (Prince's Goblet) in Osmomysla Square (near the Opera) enjoy great popularity among Lvivites.
ell-brewed coffee is served everyplace. But for some reason it tastes best in cozy coffee shops which are in abundant supply.
ell-ground coffee, brewed Turkish-style on roasted sand is the popular choice. It tastes best with cool mineral water or
gnac. You can smoke wherever there are ashtrays on the tables.
ost restaurants and cafes serve customers until 11 p.m., which is more than enough to eat and drink one's fill.
Lviv's old center there are a number of outlets where food is quite inexpensive, though it does not mean that it is not
licious. It's only that you will have to serve yourself, and there are more visitors. The dishes are simple, helpings are
eable. In a word, these are people's outlets. Among them are Domova Kukhnya (Home Cuisine) mockingly dubbed
movyna, opposite George Hotel and a canteen in the right wing of the City Hall in Rynok Square.
ditional Halychan cuisine has a number of dishes which can be tasted nowhere else but Lviv. These are: Chanakhy, once an
clusive traditional Tatar dish of meat, kidney beans, potatoes, garlic, all braised in an earthenware pot. Rubtsi, specially treated
ces of cow stomach prepared with spicy sauce. Bigos, sauerkraut, braised with meat and prunes. Kryzhavky, sliced up cabbage,
ured with beetroot and seasoned with grated garlic... All those hotdogs and hamburgers do not hold a candle to the above dishes!
t chefs of each cuisine have their own culinary gems, scrumptious only if prepared by them and nobody else. Bon appetite!

Краєзнавчий фотонарис
ТІЛЬКИ У ЛЬВОВІ
Мандрівки древнім містом
(англійською мовою)

Видання друге, доповнене

Текст	— Олесь Ганущак
Світлини	— Йосиф Марухняк
Керівник проекту, редактор	— Святослав Яворівський
Комп'ютерний дизайн	— Галина Горбачук
Переклад	— Лінгвістичний центр (перекладачі Ігор Саповський, Олена Ржепецька)

ISBN 966-8013-46-8

Свідоцтво про внесення до державного реєстру
ДК № 618 від 02.10.2001 р.

Повне товариство — видавнича фірма «Афіша».
м. Львів, вул. Замарстинівська, 53.
Тел./факс: (0322) 966-510, 97-14-27.

Віддруковано ПТВФ «Афіша».
м. Львів, вул. Замарстинівська, 53.